Greenwich Community College
235492
D0590092

NEW TECHNOLOGY

medical technology

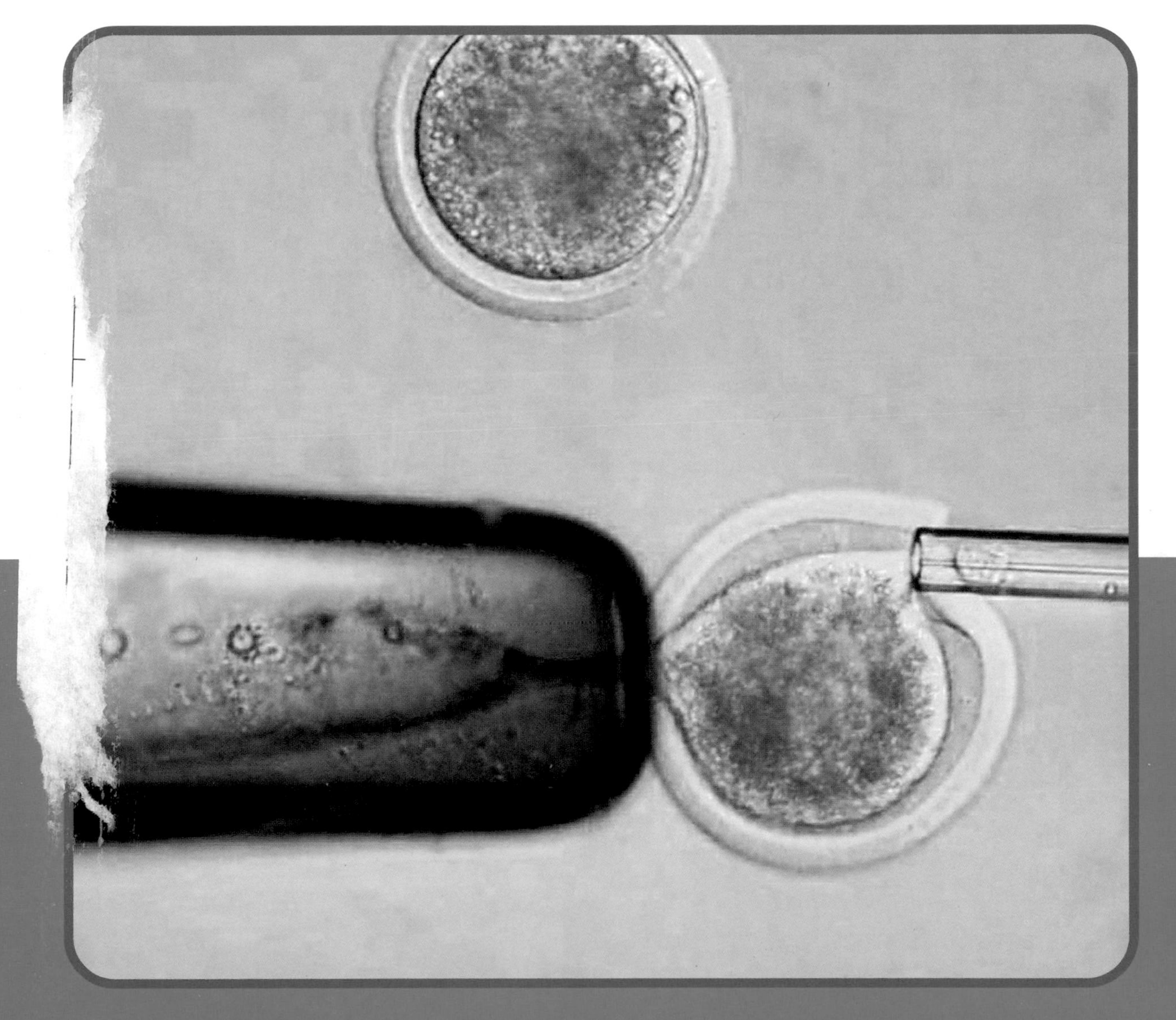

Robert Snedden

Greenwich Community College
London

Acc No. 235492
Class No 610 SNE
Date on System 2/2/11 AA.

Published by Evans Brothers Limited

© 2008 Evans Brothers Ltd

Evans Brothers Limited
2A Portman Mansions
Chiltern Street
London W1U 6NR

First published 2008

All rights reserved. No part of this publication may be reproduced, stored in a retrieval system, or transmitted, in any form or by any means, electronic, mechanical, photocopying, recording or otherwise, without the prior permission of Evans Brothers Limited.

British Library Cataloguing
in Publication Data
Snedden, Robert
Medical technology. - (New technology)
1. Medical innovations - Juvenile
Literature
2. Title
610

ISBN 978 0 2375 3427 1

Printed in China

Credits
Series Editor: Paul Humphrey
Editor: Gianna Williams
Designer: Keith Williams
Production: Jenny Mulvanny
Picture researchers: Rachel Tisdale
and Laura Embriaco
Consultant: Matthew Clemence BSc Phd,
Research Scientist, Philips Medical Systems

Acknowledgements
Title page: RBM Online/Reuters/Corbis; p.6 Master Sgt. Kimberley Spencer/U. S. Air Force; p.7 Don Bayley/istockphoto.com; pp.8-9 Matthew Clemence/Philips Medical Systems; p.10 Charles Ommanney/Getty Images; p.11 Fraunhofer IPA; p.12 Joseph Hitt; p.13 Otto Bock; p.14 University of Southern California/National Science Foundation; p.15 Cochlear Ltd; p.16 3DClinic/Getty Images; p.17 Dan McCoy/Rainbow/Getty Images; p.18 Schrodinger, LLC; p.19 Brian Sullivan/Visuals Unlimited/Getty Images; p.20 Roger Ressmeyer/Corbis; p.21 top Mediscan/Corbis; p.21 bottom David Umberger/Purdue University; p.22 Alex Bennett/istockphoto.com; p.23 Dr. David Phillips/Visuals Unlimited/Getty Images; p.25 Vo Trung Du/Corbis Sygma; p.26 Getty Images; p.27 Bio Sidus/Reuters/Corbis; p.28 Kat Wade/San Francisco Chronicle/Corbis; p.30 Robert Sciarrino/ Star Ledger/Corbis; p.31Chris Stewart/San Francisco Chronicle/Corbis; p.32 Rafael Diaz/EFE/Corbis; p.33 Norman Chan/istockphoto.com; p.34 RBM Online/Reuters/Corbis; p.35 EPA/Corbis; p.36 University of Michigan; p.37 Randy Montoya/Sandia National Laboratories; p.38 Randy Montoya/Sandia National Laboratories; pp.40-41 Ecole Polytechnique de Montreal/Nanorobotics Laboratory; p.42 Fred Hutchinson Cancer Research Center; p.43 Siemens.

This book was prepared for Evans Brothers Ltd by Discovery Books Ltd.

contents

Integrated Learning Resources Centre
Greenwich Community College
95 Plumstead Road
London SE18 7DQ

introduction

We can all dream of being in a world where disease and injury are dealt with as quickly and as painlessly as possible, or where disease is prevented altogether. Although a world without the pain of injury and illness will probably never be possible, medical science has made stunning advances in that direction in the last few years.

A better, longer life Thanks to developments in medical technology, combined with other factors such as better nutrition, people are living longer than ever. In the developed world, the age group of the very old – over 80 years of age – is the fastest-growing population group.

At the other end of the scale, infant mortality has also been reduced drastically. In October 2006 a baby born at just 21 weeks and six days and weighing 10 ounces became the world's youngest baby to survive. This miracle baby exists thanks entirely to medical technology. Apart from the

Nurses specialised in bone marrow transplants explain the procedure to a patient at Wilford Hall Medical Centre, Lackland Air Force Base, Texas, USA.

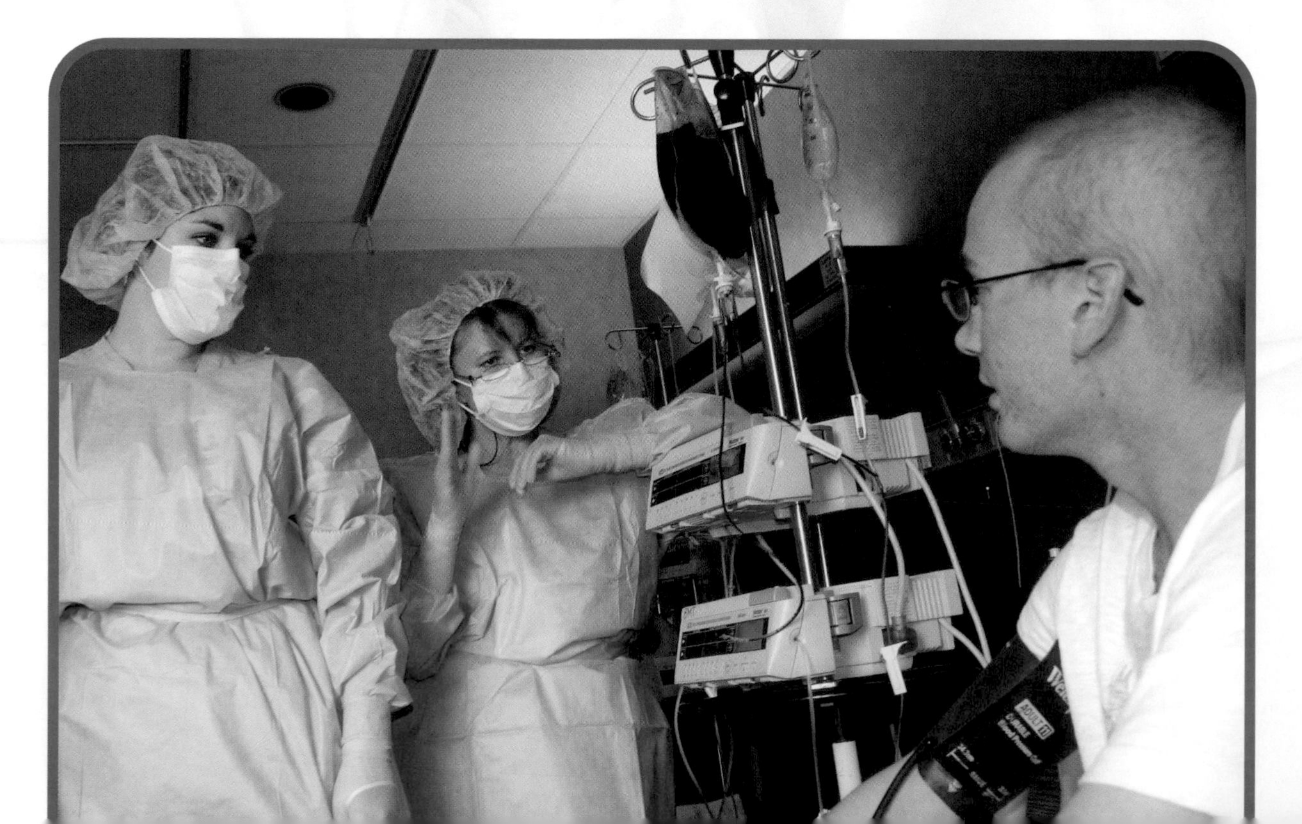

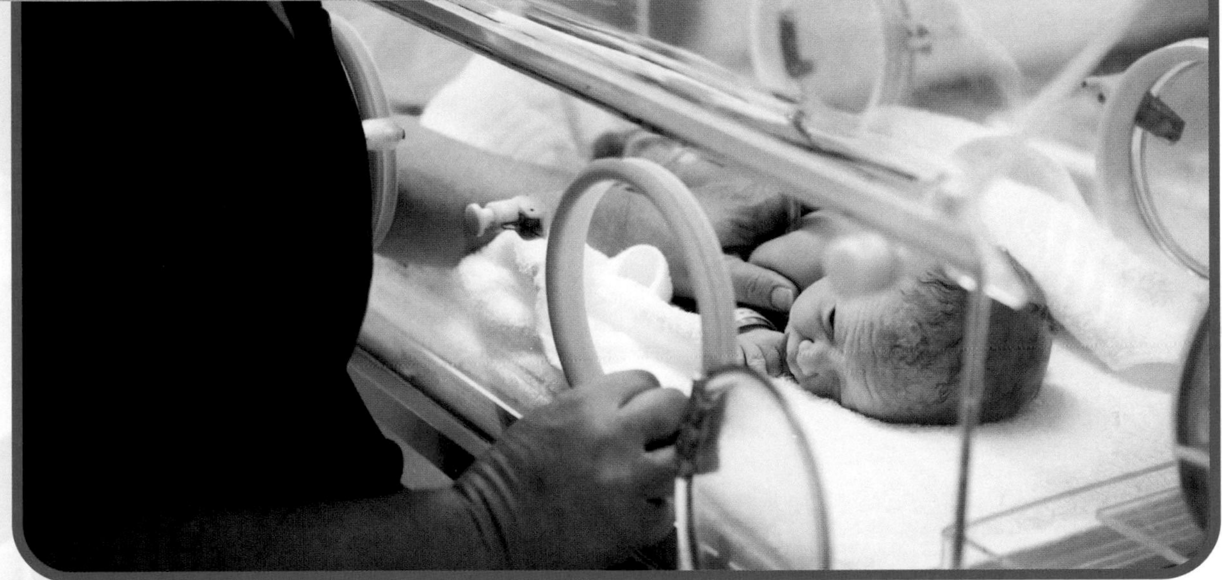

Improved systems for keeping premature babies alive have forced doctors to reconsider how old a baby has to be to be considered 'viable' – able to survive without suffering serious health problems in the future.

incubators that kept her alive once she was born, she had been conceived through IVF treatment.

New technology We are now on the edge of even greater developments with unlimited possibilities for preventing and curing disease. Discoveries in genetics (the study of the ways in which characteristics are passed from parents to offspring), for example, have opened up whole new fields of medicine.

We can now see what is happening inside a body without having to perform surgery. Even our thoughts and emotions can now be caught, as it were, on film thanks to new scanners that are being developed.

Advances in technology are helping to restore sight and hearing to people, and to bring movement and ability back for people who have lost limbs. Some of these developments are taking place on the cutting edge of technology down in the nanoscale, where things are measured in atoms and molecules.

Controversies Marvellous though these breakthroughs are, they are not simple or straightforward to accomplish. Sometimes, as with the controversies surrounding genetics and stem cell research, there are problems to be solved that are not purely medical. As well as looking at how the technology works and the benefits it can bring, we will also look at some of the problems involved in its use, such as the costs involved in designing drugs for individuals or the moral issues that are raised by stem cell research.

CHAPTER 1
seeing inside

Often in the past surgeons have had to perform surgery on people without being absolutely sure what was wrong with them. There was no way of looking inside someone's body without cutting it open.

Now with the help of advanced technology, doctors and surgeons can see what is going on inside a person's body. Magnetic resonance imaging (or MRI) has very quickly established itself as an important tool in medicine. Unlike an X-ray, which only sees bones, an MRI scan allows doctors to look at soft tissues inside the body.

A modern MRI scanner, driven by powerful computers, can produce many thousands of images at a speed fast enough to freeze motion. This means that doctors can watch movement inside the body, even a beating heart.

In recent years, even more powerful systems have become available and the extra power they have allows very detailed images of the brain to be collected. A new technique, called

Whole body Tesla 7 MRI scanners first became available in 2001.

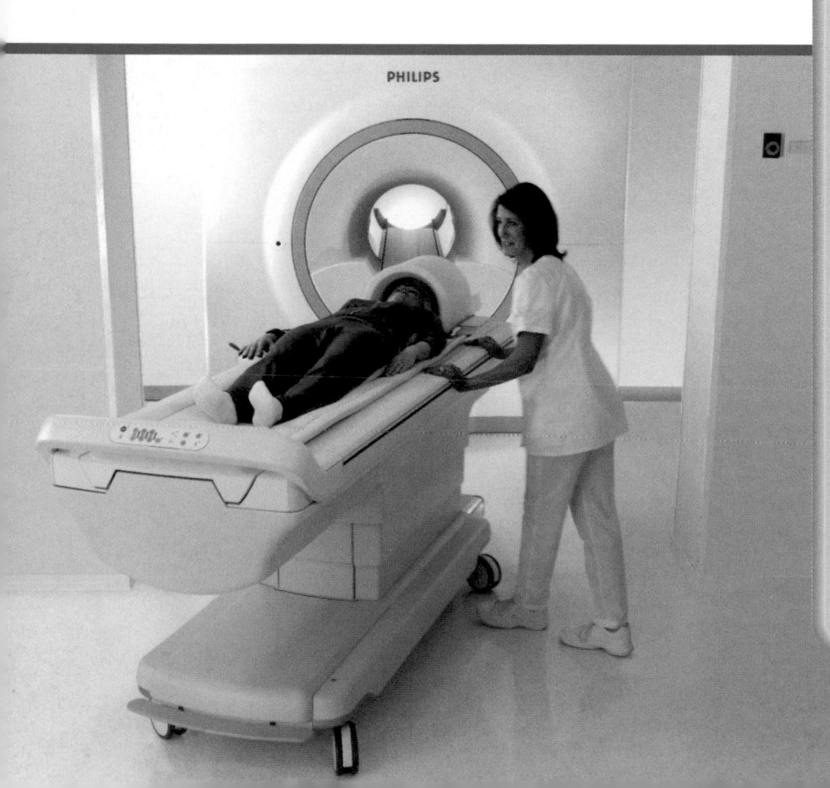

HOW IT WORKS

An MRI scanner looks at the water content of the human body, or more specifically the hydrogen atoms in the water. Water is not normally magnetic, but by using very large magnetic fields (a typical hospital scanner has a magnet of 1.5 Teslas, or 30,000 times the Earth's magnetic field) hydrogen atoms in the body can be made to emit very tiny radio signals. As these signals pass straight through the body, their position can be accurately mapped and a detailed image produced.

functional MRI (fMRI), can detect the very small changes in blood supply which happen when a part of the brain has to work harder, for example if someone is asked to tap their fingers. For complex tasks, such as recognising faces, language – or even lying – fMRI helps scientists understand how the brain works and recovers from injury, and may help in planning and testing future treatments.

MEG The inner workings of the brain have long fascinated scientists and philosophers. Techniques such as MRI give superbly detailed pictures of the brain, but tell you little about how it works. Now MEG (Magneto-encephalography) is helping scientists discover the innermost workings of the brain. The communications between nerve cells generate a small but measurable magnetic field. Using several hundred SQUIDs – Superconducting QUantum Interference Devices, extremely sensitive magnetic detectors – these fields can be measured and also located within the brain. If you decide to tap your finger on a table, many parts of the brain are used – some to control the muscles, some to receive the sense of touch, others to interpret that touch as a tap on wood perhaps. SQUIDs act very quickly and allow you to say exactly when such actions happened in the brain, though they can't tell you exactly where. However, combined with functional MRI, someday scientists may even be able to find the place in the brain where the decision was first made.

The use of MEG also has other benefits. At the moment, researchers who want to study conditions such as epilepsy will study rodents and monkeys whose brains have been damaged on purpose to mimic these human systems. With MEG, such animal experiments could no longer be necessary.

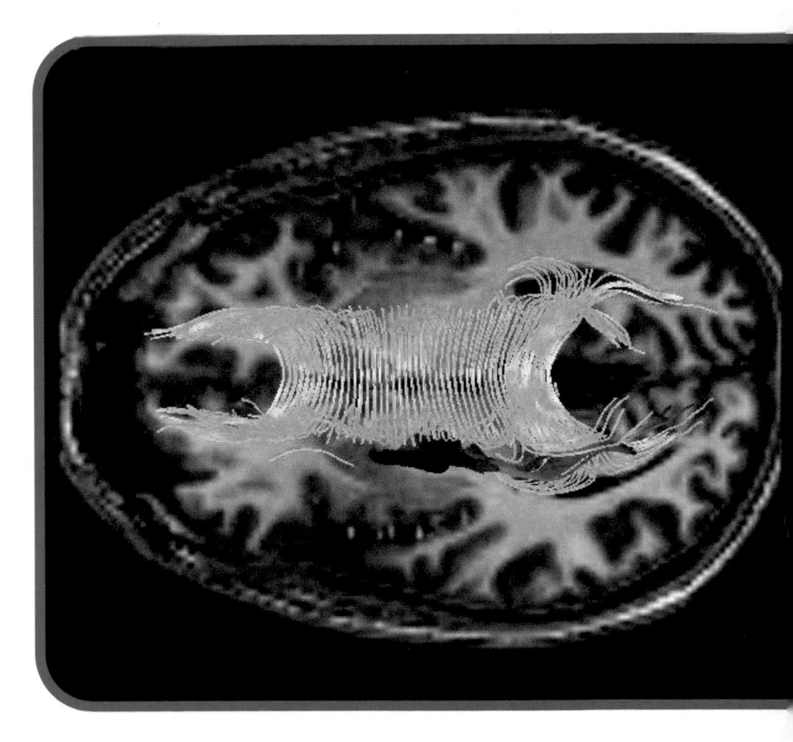

The dark blue area on this MRI scan shows a thought as it crosses the brain. Recent improvements in scanners allow doctors to 'see' a thought process as it happens.

CHAPTER 2
we can rebuild you

Artificial limbs, also called prostheses, have come a long way in the last few years. At present, an artificial limb is attached to what remains of the missing limb using an external socket. But that may become a thing of the past within the next few years.

Point of attachment Researchers at University College London (UCL), England, have recently developed a technique that involves inserting a titanium rod into the patient's bone. The rod extends through the skin, which grows around it forming a seal that prevents bacteria entering the body. The artificial limb can then be attached directly to the titanium rod. Skin is a barrier to infection so the skin needs to grow around the metal rod. To work out how to do this, scientists from the Centre for Biomedical Engineering at UCL turned to the deer.

A patient undergoes a check-up of his prosthetic arm in San Diego, California, in February 2007.

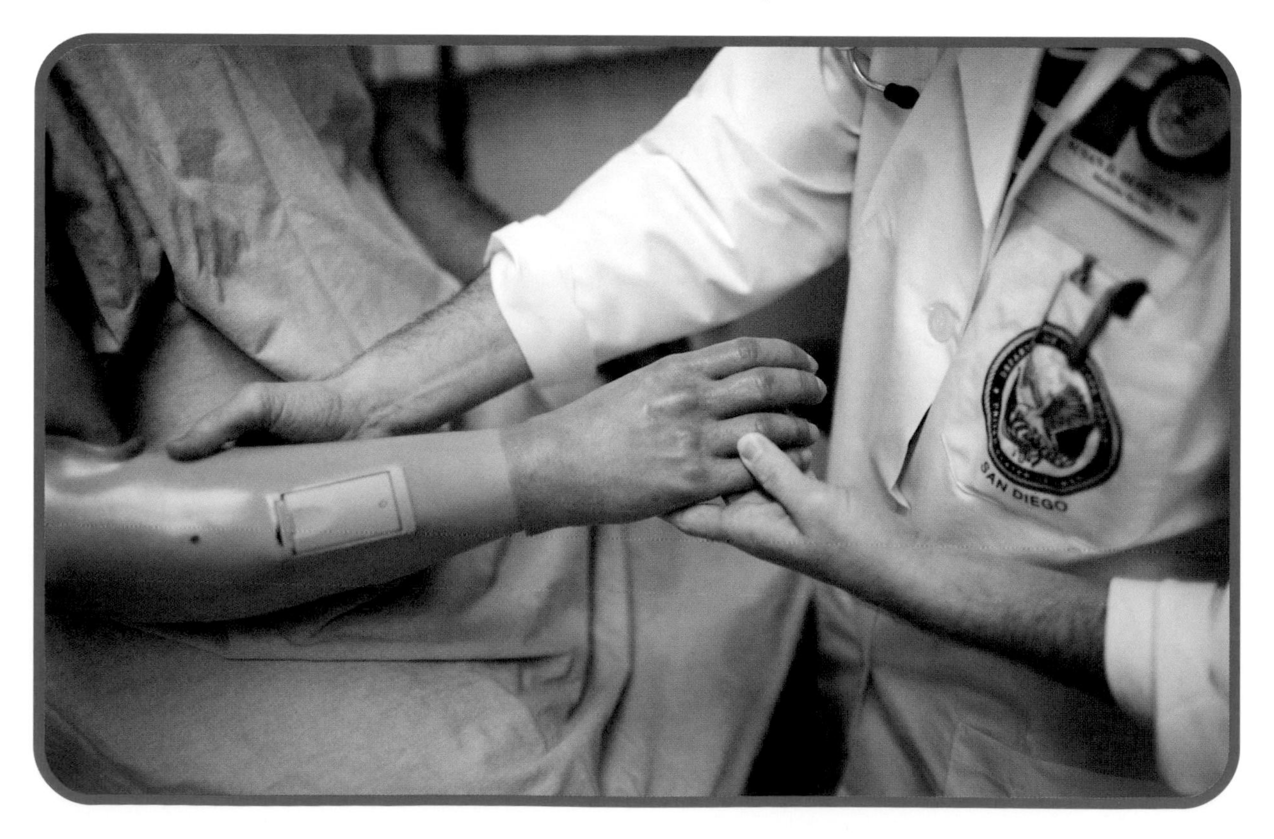

A deer's antlers can grow through the animal's skin without infection. The researchers mimicked the design of the bone in a deer's antlers when they made the titanium pins.

Early clinical trials at Mount Vernon Hospital, Middlesex, have been carried out on a small group of patients who had lost fingers or thumbs. The results have been promising. The next stage will be to carry out trials on upper and lower limb replacements. In just a few years the technology could be widely used to replace lost limbs.

Elephant's trunk to robot arm

Researchers at the Fraunhofer Institute in Stuttgart have used the suppleness and agility of an elephant's trunk as a design model for a bionic robot arm. The human arm is incredibly complex, consisting of many bones, muscles and nerves which it is impossible to reproduce exactly with current technology. By mimicking nature, where two muscles always work together to produce an action, a new arm, called ISELLA, is different. Whereas earlier arms had a single motor to move each joint, ISELLA has pairs of motors. If one fails, the other takes over, preventing uncontrolled movements of the arm. Just as tendons in the body attach one muscle to another, cords link moving parts in ISELLA. A drive shaft is attached to the midpoint of each cord and when this turns, the cord wraps around it, pulling the joints together. This has proved to be a much cheaper and more effective system than using gears. The ISELLA robot arm has ten of these 'muscles' and is as flexible as a human arm. At present the research team is working to perfect the arm's elbow.

SPARKy Much of the research carried out into producing better and better artificial limbs has come about as a result of the needs of military personnel injured in combat. Researchers from the Walter Reed Army Medical Centre and Arizona State

The mechanics in ISELLA, normally enclosed in a padded sleeve. Similar devices could be commercially available by 2010.

A volunteer tries SPARKy out on a treadmill. SPARKy is still in its testing phase.

HOW IT WORKS

When you walk, as your heel strikes the ground energy is stored in the tendons around your ankle. This is released as your foot lifts. In SPARKy a tuned spring stores the energy. A lightweight motor is used to adjust the position of the spring, just as you unconsciously adjust the position of your ankle as you walk.

University in the USA have created a device, nicknamed SPARKy – short for Spring Ankle with Regenerative Kinetics. It will be a lower leg replacement that is based on lightweight energy-storing springs. With existing technology in limb replacement, the amputees have to use 20 to 30 per cent more energy to propel themselves forward when walking compared to an able-bodied person. SPARKy's springs will provide the 'push-off power' that an able-bodied person gets naturally. All being well, SPARKy should be ready for everyday use by 2009.

C-leg Another of the Walter Reed Army Medical Centre's breakthroughs is the the C-leg. C-legs, made of graphite and titanium, are battery-powered artificial limbs with built-in microprocessors to improve control of movement, making them much more stable than previous artificial legs. The C-leg is fitted with computerised sensors that can read the strain applied to the leg 50 times a second, then make rapid adjustments to the user's stride to allow the leg to adapt quickly to different walking speeds.

When a person is first fitted with a C-leg, a computer is used to program the knee system to match the way the patient normally walks.

Myoelectric hands No matter how good an artifical limb is, it is useless if the person who needs it cannot control it carefully enough to perform everyday tasks. The myoelectric hand is unique because of its ability to function with the user's own muscle movements. Myoelectric hands can open and close with quick movements so that the user can grab and grip as with a normal hand. Whenever a muscle in the body is contracted, a small electrical signal called an EMG is created by a chemical interaction in the body. Electrodes attached to the surface of the skin detect the EMG signal, amplify it, and then pass it on to a controller that switches on and off the motors that control the movement of the artificial hand or arm to produce movement and function.

This is what a myoelectric hand looks like on the inside, as it holds a microchip.

Bionic eyes In 2007 medical researchers succeeded in creating some amazing miniaturised implants that could return sight to many people in the not-too-distant future. These implants are designed for the treatment of blindness due to eye diseases that damage the retina, the light-gathering part of the eye. The disease affects the cells in the retina that capture and process light, causing loss of vision.

The parts of the 'bionic eye'. The whole thing is powered by a battery pack that can be clipped to the waist along with the video processor in a package no larger than a pager.

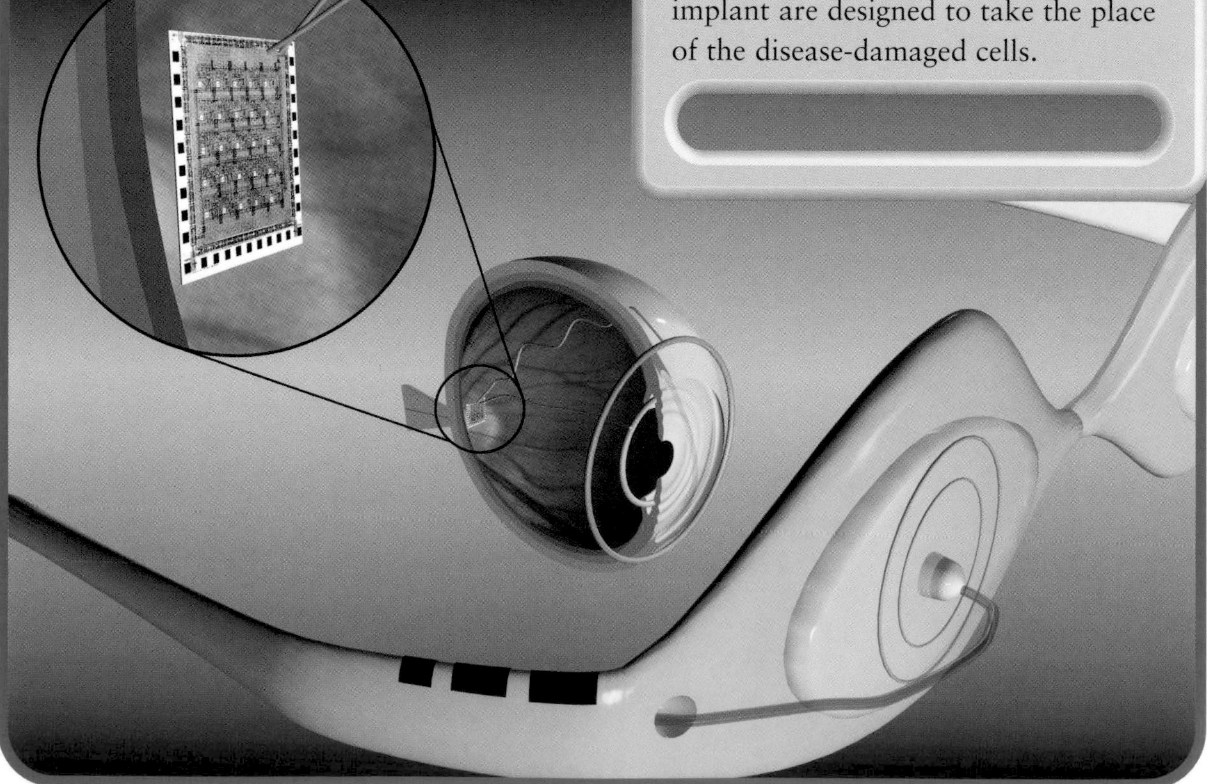

HOW IT WORKS

The 'bionic eye' consists of five main components. A small digital camera mounted on a pair of glasses captures images; these are then sent to a video-processing microchip that converts the images into electrical pulses representing light and dark areas in the image; the electrical pulses are sent to a radio transmitter that is also fitted to the glasses; the radio transmitter sends pulses to a receiver that is implanted above the wearer's ear; the radio receiver sends the pulses down a hair-thin wire to a tiny electronic implant that is attached to the retina of the eye. Electrodes mounted in the implant are designed to take the place of the disease-damaged cells.

If trials of the retinal implant are successful it could be available for wide use by 2010. The current implant only has 60 electrodes, which is only enough for very limited vision, allowing the wearer to distinguish between shapes. Researchers are already planning a 1,000-electrode version that they believe will allow the wearer to recognise different faces.

Smart prostheses The retinal implant is part of a new class of artificial aids called 'smart prostheses'. These devices link up with the patient's brain and nervous system to restore function that has been lost through disease or injury. Another example is the cochlear implant. This is a small electronic device that can help to provide a sense of sound to a deaf person. It works in a similar way to the retinal implant. A microphone picks up sounds from the environment and sends them to a speech processor that selects and arranges the sounds. These are then sent via a transmitter to a receiver that converts them into electrical impulses and sends them to a number of electrodes linked to the auditory nerve, which transmits sound to the brain.

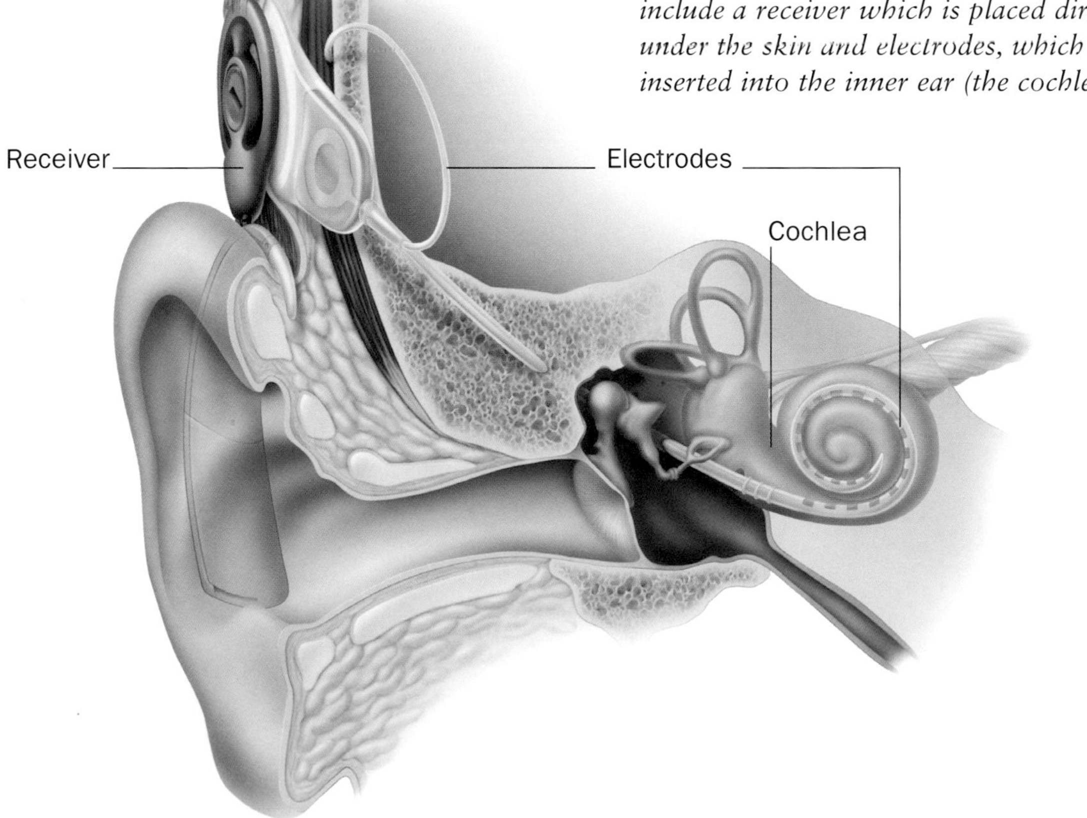

The internal parts of the cochlear implant include a receiver which is placed directly under the skin and electrodes, which are inserted into the inner ear (the cochlea).

CHAPTER 3
designer drugs

Why is it that some people take a medicine and it does them good, while other people take the same medicine for the same problem, and have no benefit at all? Why is it that some people actually get worse if they take that same medicine? The answer lies in our genes.

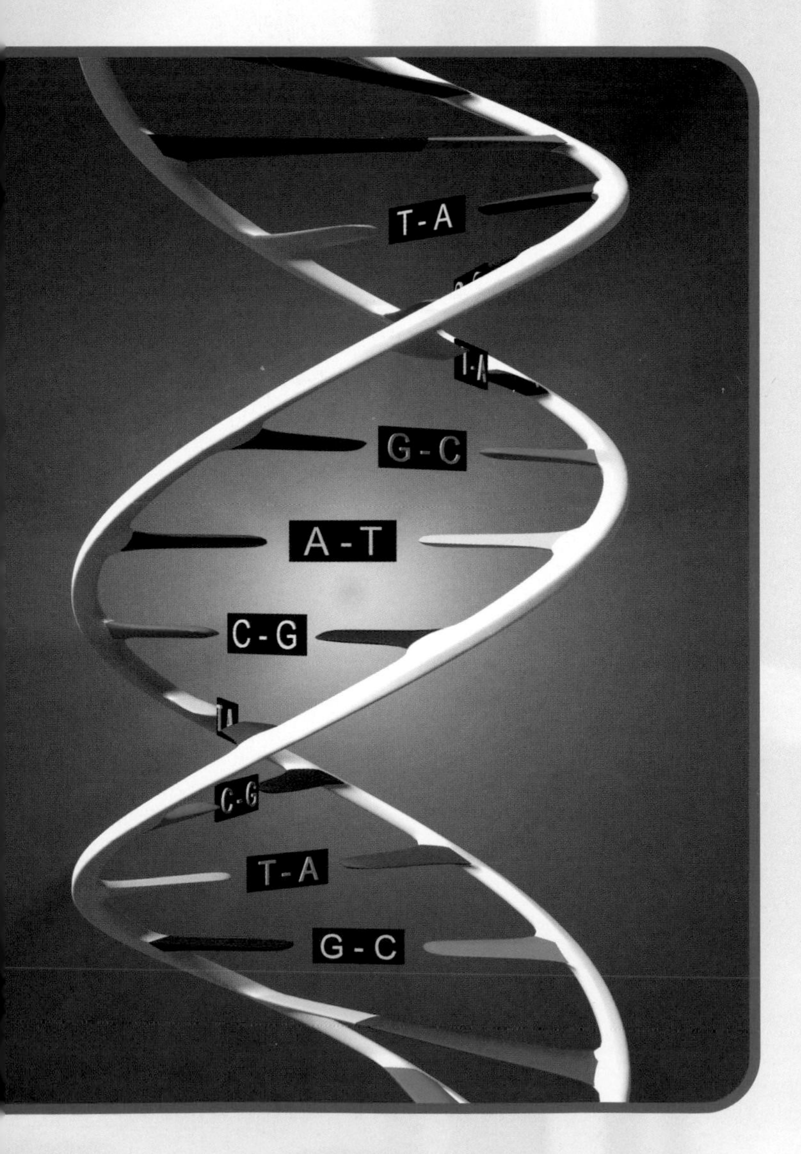

The structure of DNA. The chemicals that make up the 'teeth' on this 'zip' are often represented by the letters A, G, C and T.

People have always known that children tend to look like their parents, with bits seeming to come from either father or mother, but all mixed up to create a new individual. How this could happen wasn't known until the discovery of a complex molecule called DNA. This molecule, which is found inside almost every cell in the body, is formed of two strands, like the two sides of a zip, which fit together exactly. Each tooth of the zip is one of four chemicals. Encoded in the entire length of the DNA molecule is all of the information which is passed on from parent to child – known as the genome. The study of how these molecules affect the body is called genetics.

Some of the greatest advances in medical care will come from our increasing knowledge of genetics. Genes produce the molecules which form and run the cells in our bodies. These genes are turned on and off all the time as part of how the body functions. However many diseases are caused by genes being activated or deactivated at the wrong times. Not only that, but the way in which our bodies respond to treatments also depends on our genes as they also control how our bodies defend themselves from disease.

Pharmacogenetics While we all share the bulk of our DNA code – because we are all human beings – we all have our own small variations which make us unique. In fact, if medicines work better in some people than others it is probably due to these differences. Pharmacogenetics uses a knowledge of genetics to predict the safety and effectiveness of a drug. A person's genes play a big part in determining how he or she will react to different medicines. Sometimes a medicine that is effective for one person will have no effect on another. For example, codeine, a common painkiller, is totally ineffective in ten per cent of the population. Some drugs that work for most people may have nasty side effects for others. In the

WHAT'S NEXT?

In the future your medical records might include a catalogue of your genes. It may be that one day, in the not-too-distant future, you can have your own personal genome sequenced and any treatment you might need will be tailored exactly to your genetic code. This is already possible, but extremely expensive.

A researcher extracts DNA from a sample in a test tube. Studying a person's DNA helps to understand why they develop certain diseases.

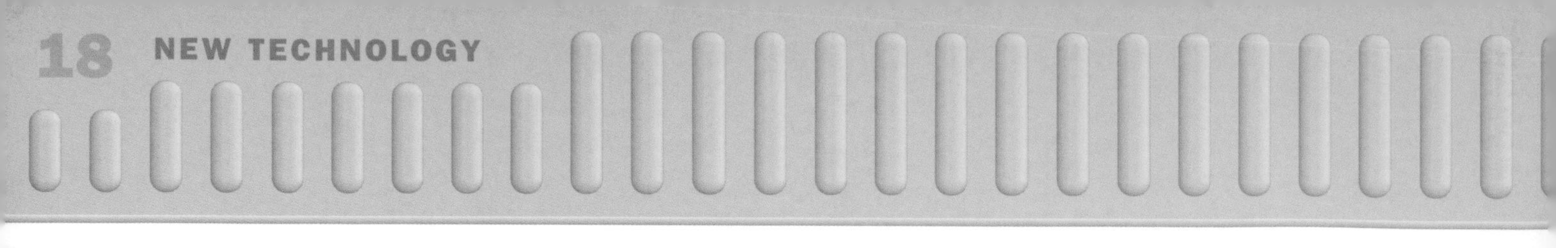

US alone, two million people each year become ill because of bad reactions to drugs they have been given. Many of them even die. Knowing what is right for a particular patient can save time and money and help the person get well faster.

Enzymes Substances called enzymes are a type of protein that controls the rates of the various chemical reactions in your body. Researchers are particularly interested in enzymes that deal with reactions involving drugs. Some people don't have the enzyme needed to break down a particular drug, so if they take medication containing it, the drug will build up in the body, causing a bad reaction. Others might have an enzyme that breaks the drug down so rapidly that it has no time to take effect, so they get no benefit from taking that medicine. Since genes determine the proteins present in your body, including enzymes, genes also determine how your body reacts to different drugs.

Computers and drug design

The ways in which drugs react in the body are extremely complex. Designing a new drug can be hard work, both time-consuming and expensive. Usually tens of thousands of compounds have to be tested to find a promising new drug and only very few of these will get as far as full-scale testing on human volunteers.

More and more, researchers are turning to powerful computers to help design new drugs. Producing computer models of human cells and tissue is seen

A computer-generated image of an anti-cancer drug. How a new drug will act can often be determined by looking at the shape of its molecules, just as pieces of a jigsaw fit together.

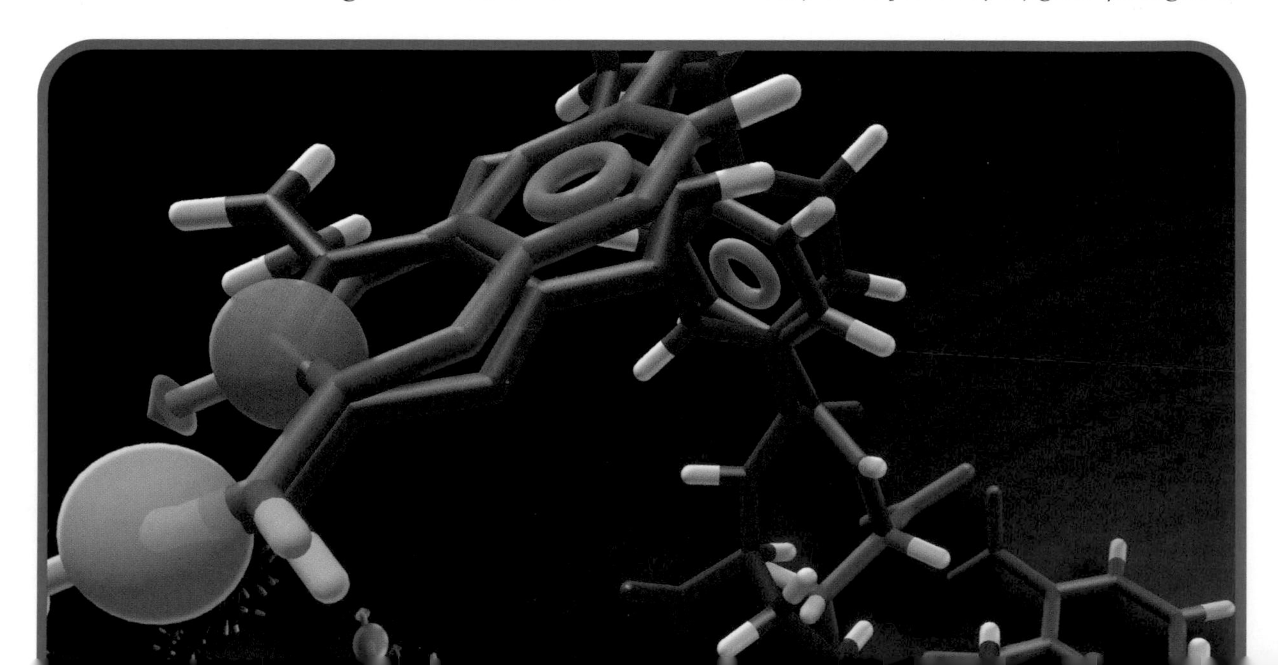

WHAT'S NEXT?

Researchers in Singapore and China have used computer-aided drug design to test a new drug for schistosomiasis. This is a serious illness that can lead to liver failure and is caused by a flatworm that enters through the victim's skin. It affects 200 million people in developing regions all over the world, particularly in China. The drug is now waiting for a patent before it can be used commercially.

A close-up of the schistosomiasis flat worm, taken with an electron microscope. Computers are helping to produce drugs that kill this parasite.

as a cost-effective and efficient way of predicting how a drug will react in the body. In addition, running computer simulations can be carried out as often as necessary before an actual drug is produced. The researcher can establish early on whether the drug should be adopted, adapted or abandoned.

In drug development, researchers make computer models of the drugs and also the molecules in the body that the drugs interact with. The idea is to design a tight fit between the two, so drugs can be made that are precisely and effectively targeted. This requires the use of powerful computers and computer programs capable of rendering complex three-dimensional models.

Model humans Software is now available that can construct whole populations of human beings that exist only on the computer. These can have all the variations of disease, genetics, age ranges and so on that are found in a real human population. This software allows drug companies to test their computer-generated drug designs over a wide range of possible patients. This approach has been used, for example, to determine drug doses for newborns and young children, something that could not be found out by testing on real subjects.

Integrated Learning Resources Centre

Scientist Michael Chaney wears special 3-D glasses to view a computer model of Fluoxetine, or Prozac, a drug taken as a tranquilliser.

Customised drugs The increasing sophistication in drug design holds out the promise that one day doctors will be able to prescribe exactly the right medicine needed to do the greatest good for each individual patient. This is the goal of pharmacogenetics – but it is still some way off. Most medicines already work well most of the time for most people. There would be huge costs involved in producing individual medicines. There may be several genes involved in a patient's response to a particular drug and it may prove difficult to untangle what is actually happening. Furthermore, genetics is not the only factor affecting the course of a disease – lifestyle and other medications the patient may be taking will have an effect.

Fighting bacteria Many illnesses happen because our body is infected by a bacterium. The very first life forms on our planet were probably bacteria-like organisms, so it is hard to fight a war against bacteria when they have had a long time to prepare their defences.

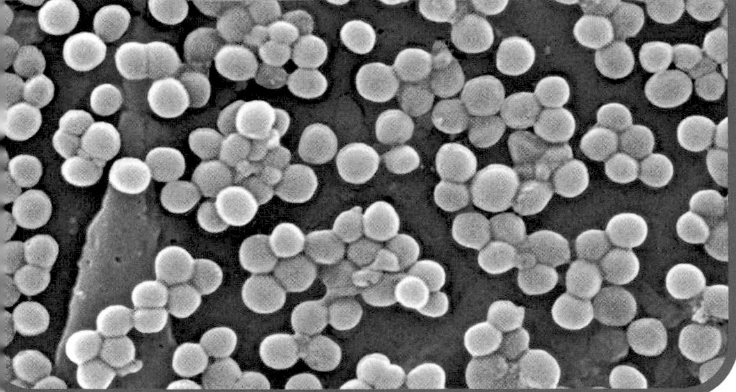

A close-up of the antibiotic-resistant bacteria Staphylococcus Aureus, also known as MRSA.

The first major step forward in the fight against bacteria was the discovery of penicillin, the first antibiotic, in the 1920s. Antibiotics are natural chemical defences produced by bacteria and fungi. Different antibiotics work in different ways on different bacteria. Some antibiotics interfere with a bacterium's ability to use energy from its food, others prevent the bacterium from reproducing.

Superbugs One of the major problems we now face is that many of the disease-causing bacteria are becoming resistant to antibiotics. Sometimes if a person fails to take a complete course of antibiotics, the most resistant bacteria survive, giving rise to a new population of stronger bacteria. Bacteria can also share genetic material amongst themselves – so one resistant bacterium can pass its ability on to another.

A researcher passes laser light through a colony of bacteria. The patterns caused by light help identify what types of bacteria they are.

Bioprospecting Researchers are on the look-out for new antibiotics. Looking for natural substances produced by living things that might be of benefit in medicine is called bioprospecting. In the past there has been a very 'hit and miss' approach to this, with samples being taken from many thousands of organisms in the hope that one will pay dividends. Now scientists can use genetics to quickly identify good candidates for new drugs.

The counterattack: LexA In 2005, biochemist Floyd Romesberg of the Scripps Research Institute in California, discovered that bacteria have a gene, called LexA, that triggers their DNA into rapidly mutating. Romesberg has learned how to turn off LexA. After screening 100,000 possible compounds he discovered a molecule that works against LexA's ability to cause mutations. The molecule can enter the bacteria's cells easily to reach their DNA.

This new compound won't prevent bacterial infections. It will be taken along with antibiotics, and will prevent bacteria from mutating in response to antibiotics, and so prevent new resistant strains from developing. The compound might also give new life to older antibiotics that have stopped working. Romesberg's lab is also looking for ways to stop the mutations that cause cancer.

A crowded beehive might be a good place to go bioprospecting.

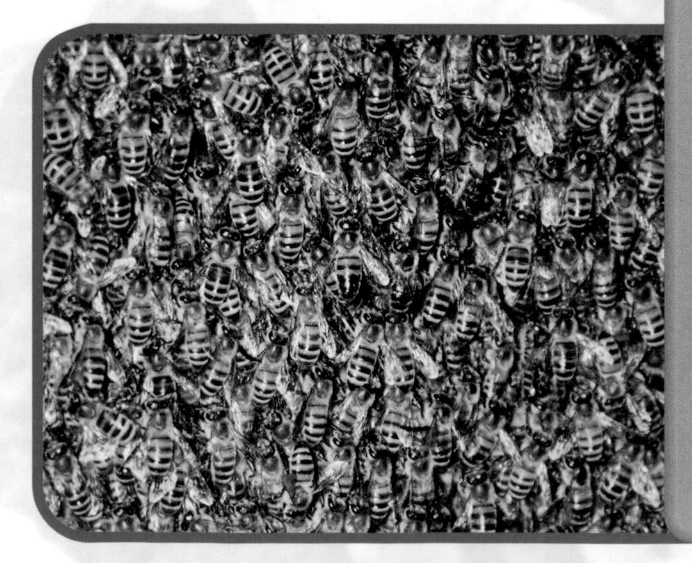

WHAT'S NEXT?

New research being carried out at Macquarie University in Australia is looking at beehives in the hope of discovering new antibiotics. A crowded beehive is a very good place for disease to spread quickly from one bee to the next, so bees have evolved ways of preventing this. One of the most effective methods they have is to produce a substance that acts as a barrier to infection. The researchers hope that the bee defences against bacteria will open the way to developing stronger and more effective antibiotics.

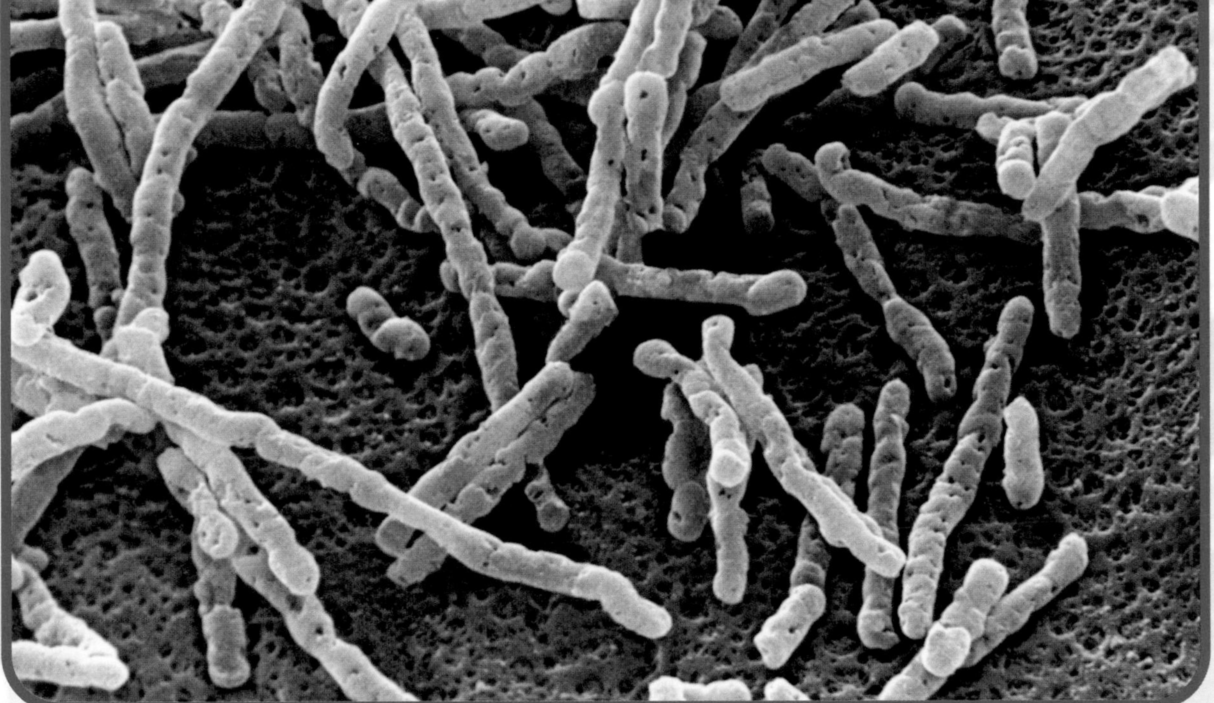

An electron-microscopic view of the Clostridium bacteria.

A knockout: ClosTron It sounds like something from a science fiction movie, but the ClosTron knockout system could be one of the major weapons we have in the fight against disease. One of the deadliest of the drug-resistant superbugs is called *Clostridium difficile*, also known as C. diff. It kills three times as many people every year in the UK as the superbug MRSA.

In 2007 scientists at the University of Nottingham developed the ClosTron knockout system, which can target specific genes in C. diff and similar types of bacteria. The ClosTron technology switches off individual genes in the bacteria and identifies which ones are important in causing disease. If the bacteria's disease-causing capabilities have been knocked out by ClosTron, the body's natural defences will be able to deal with them quickly, reducing the need to find new antibiotics to fight the infection.

WHAT'S NEXT?

As well as knocking out genes, the ClosTron technology can be used to insert them. The researchers hope that this technique could, for example, be used to develop new anti-cancer treatments that will be delivered by the spores of harmless bacteria that target the cancer tissue.

CHAPTER 4

gene therapies and cloning

Sometimes, tiny errors in genes make us vulnerable to illness. Defects in genes are the cause of over 3,000 human diseases.

Human Genome project In 1990 many groups of scientists began to work together to map out the complete DNA code of a human being – the Human Genome project. Given that there are over three billion pieces of DNA, this was a huge undertaking and the first complete map was only produced in April 2003. The Human Genome project has already led to the discovery of more than 1,800 disease genes. Researchers can now find a gene suspected of disease in days, instead of the years it took before. There are now more than a thousand genetic tests for human diseases.

Gene therapy Genetic engineering research has reached the point where it is possible to alter a person's genes. Gene therapy is a way of treating or preventing diseases that result from faulty genes. It involves inserting 'good' genes into the patient's cells to take over from those that aren't working properly. One way of getting the replacement gene into the cells is to have it delivered in by a virus that has been genetically modified to carry the human gene.

Breakthroughs Gene therapy is already being tested on volunteers with positive results. In 2006 scientists at the National Institute of Health in Bethesda,

WHAT'S NEXT?

In 2007 scientists at the Institute of Ophthalmology at University College London and nearby Moorfields Eye Hospital began trials to find a cure for a type of blindness through gene therapy. There is a gene defect that causes the retina (the part of the eye that is sensitive to light) to stop working. People with this defect can become completely blind by the time they reach their twenties. The patients will be injected with a virus that scientists have engineered to carry a working version of the faulty gene. Once in the eye, the virus will carry the working gene into the cells of the retina. Here, the working gene will do the job that the faulty gene should have been doing and so the cells of the retina should begin to work properly. Trials carried out on dogs have shown that the treatment can work.

A researcher involved in gene therapy aimed at fighting the AIDS virus.

WHAT'S NEXT?

A new gene test can predict whether people with a particular type of lung cancer will suffer a relapse in the future. Thanks to the test, developed by the National Taiwan University College of Medicine, only those people whose genes are linked to a relapse of the cancer need undergo further chemotherapy treatment.

Maryland, USA, made an exciting breakthrough. They successfully treated two patients suffering from a type of cancer by genetically altering their killer T cells (part of the body's immune system) so that they would attack the cancer cells.

In 2007 scientists at Cornell University in New York injected a harmless virus carrying a particular gene into the brains of 12 patients suffering from Parkinson's disease. In all 12 patients, the symptoms of the disease improved by at least 25 per cent up to a year after the treatment. The gene the scientists injected makes a special enzyme that calms the area of the brain that is affected by Parkinson's.

Problems to solve Targeting specific cells in the body is difficult. In 2003 French researchers reported the successful treatment of four boys who suffered from a genetic condition that affected their immune systems. Unfortunately within a few months it was discovered that some of the new genes had been delivered to the wrong places and two of the boys had developed leukaemia.

Cloning There are always many more people in need of organ transplants than there are organs available for them. Many people's relatives are not willing to allow their organs to be transplanted when they die in hospital. Even when permission is granted to use someone's organs, they will not necessarily be suitable for transplantation. One way around this could be through a combination of genetic modification and cloning.

Pig donors The possibility is that genetically modified, cloned pigs could be used as a source of transplant organs for humans. This is because pigs are genetically very close to humans. Normally a human body will reject a pig's organ because pigs have an important gene that humans don't have. Now researchers in the United

HOW IT WORKS

Dolly the sheep was the first animal to be successfully cloned, back in 1997. She was created using a technique called somatic cell nuclear transfer. Genetic material is transferred from the nucleus of an adult donor cell to an egg from which the nucleus, containing its genetic material, has been removed. The egg containing the donor cell DNA is treated with chemicals or electric current to get it to begin to divide and grow.

These five piglets – named Noel, Angel, Star, Joy and Mary – were the first cloned pigs created especially to provide donor organs for human transplant. They were cloned by the same company that created Dolly the sheep, PPL Therapeutics.

The first successfully cloned calves from a transgenic cloned cow in Latin America, pictured in February 2004 at a Buenos Aires farm. The team of scientists said the cows' milk has a protein which might help develop medicines to prevent human diseases.

WHAT'S NEXT?

Scientists in Argentina recently succeeded in creating genetically modified, cloned calves that will produce insulin in their milk when they become cows. A herd of insulin-producing cows would reduce the cost of making insulin substantially. Twenty-five cows would produce enough to treat over a million people. The scientists hope that insulin from milk will be available for use in a year or so.

States have cloned pigs that lack a copy of this important gene.

Clones are living things that are genetically identical and they have always existed in nature. Identical twins are clones of each other because they both share the same genes. Strawberries and other plants that grow from runners are genetically identical to the parent plant. Take a cutting from a plant and grow it into a new plant and you have produced a clone.

Cloning concerns A major concern about using organs from other animals for transplantation into humans is the risk of transmitting dangerous viruses from one to the other. There is also, of course, the possibility that some people would find it distasteful on moral or religious grounds to have an animal organ in their bodies.

Transgenic cloning A transgenic organism is a living thing that has been genetically altered to have genes from another type of organism. The advantage of doing this is to create a ready source of human proteins that are medically useful. For example, almost all of the insulin used to treat diabetics comes from genetically altered bacteria that have been given the human gene responsible for producing the insulin protein.

CHAPTER 5
stem cells

Imagine a time when a person in need of a heart, or kidney, or liver transplant could simply have a new organ grown from a few cells. Imagine that any diseased or damaged tissue in the body could be repaired quickly and easily. This is the future for stem cell therapy.

What are stem cells? A stem cell is a cell that has the potential to become any other type of cell. You started life as a single cell that divided to form an embryo – a collection of cells that were all the same. These embryonic cells are stem cells. As the embryo grows, the stem cells can develop into any of the different types of cell – nerve cells, blood cells, muscle, skin and so on –

Colonies of hundreds of human embryonic stem cells in a serum of nutrients are placed under the microscope at VistaGen in Burlingame, California, USA. Here stem cells are used to study cures for diabetes.

WHAT'S NEXT?

Scientists at the Tokyo University of Science in Japan have succeeded in growing teeth from cells. The cells were taken from mouse embryos, then grown as tooth buds and finally implanted into the mouths of adult mice, where they grew as healthy teeth. The researchers now hope to do the same for humans using stem cells.

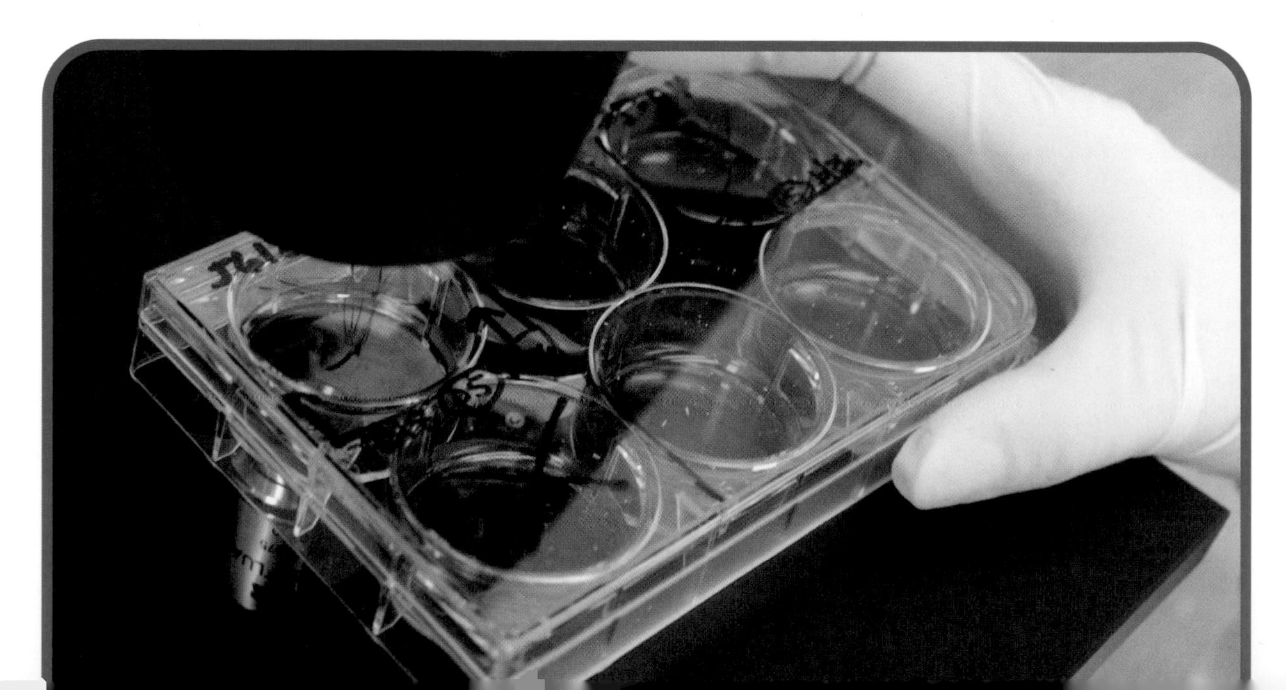

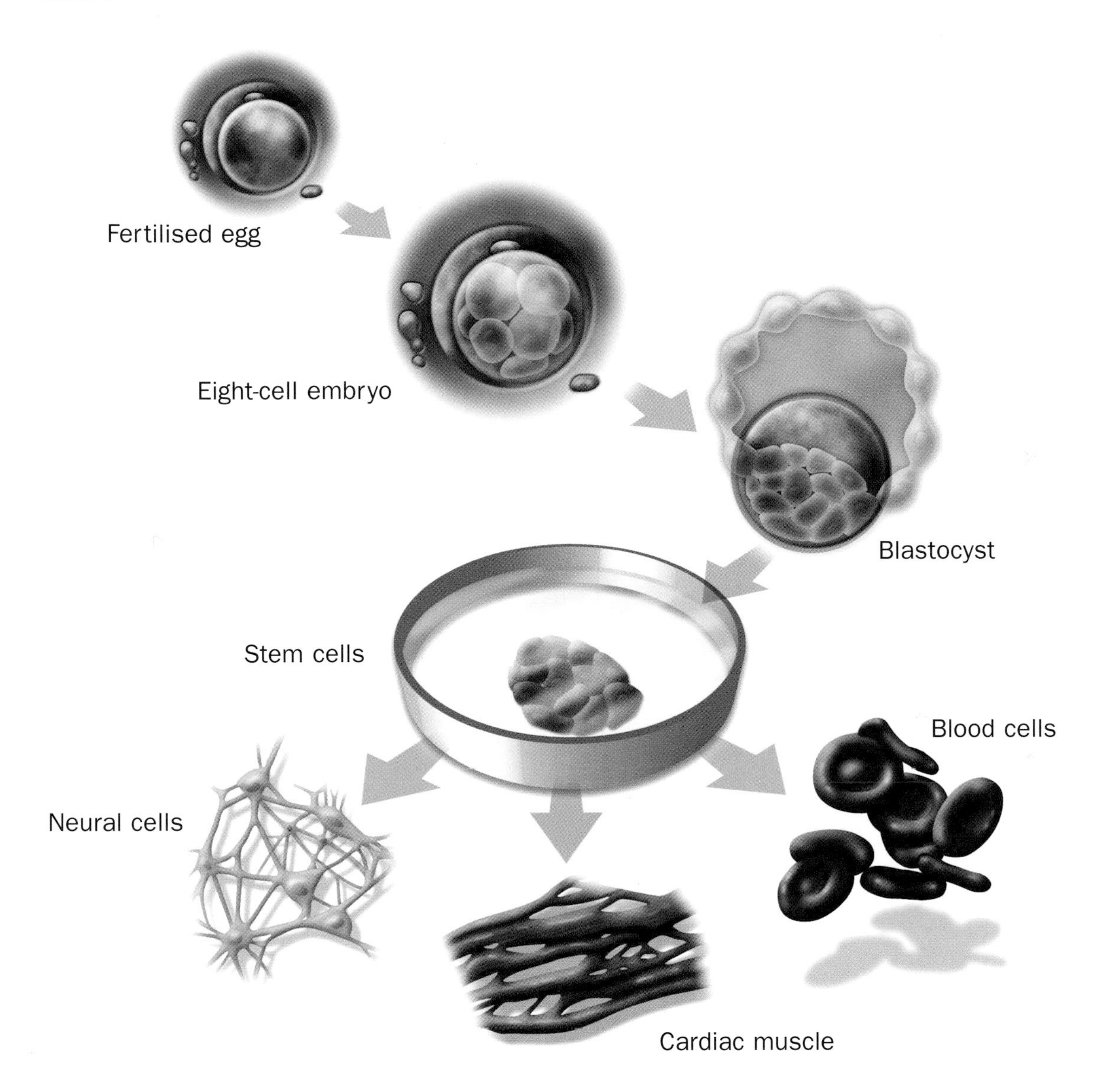

How an egg develops after fertilisation. Stem cells develop at the blastocyst stage, and then later change into the different types of cells in the body.

that form your body. Stem cells are found in different tissues in the body throughout life. These specialised stem cells are ready to divide and replace cells that are lost through natural wear and tear.

Stem cell research Stem cells are found throughout the body, as well as in umbilical cords, and form part of the body's natural repair system. However these cells are limited in the different types of tissues that they can turn into. Instead the cells of an embryo can turn into the whole human body. These embryonic stem cells are the most flexible and can be obtained from a fertilised egg just a few days old. At this stage the embryo consists of around a hundred cells and forms a spherical structure called a blastocyst. Each blastocyst has an outer layer of cells surrounding a fluid-filled cavity. At one end of this cavity there is a group of about 30 stem cells. This is called the inner cell mass and it will form all of the cells in the body.

Scientists remove the inner cell mass and transfer it to a specially treated plastic dish. Here the cells divide. As the dish fills up with cells some are removed to form fresh cell cultures on other dishes. Eventually the researchers will have many millions of cells for study. If the cells are still dividing successfully after six months and haven't developed into other cell types, they are referred to as an embryonic stem cell line. Researchers first succeeded in doing this in 1998. At present most of the stem cells used in research come from human embryos

WHAT'S NEXT?

Stem cells have helped dogs with muscular dystrophy to walk again. Duchenne muscular dystrophy is caused by mutations in a gene and affects dogs and humans. Scientists at the San Raffaele Scientific Institute in Milan, Italy used gene therapy on golden retrievers affected by the disease. Repeated doses of cells from healthy donors restored muscle function in four out of five dogs. The team hopes to begin trials on humans soon.

A lab supervisor at LifebankUSA transfers stem sells from an umbilical cord into a special deep freeze storage bag in October 2006. LifebankUSA allows parents to store stem cells for future use.

left over from infertility treatments.

Stem cells are also found in the placenta, in the amniotic fluid that surrounds the developing foetus and in the umbilical cord. Cord blood may be collected at birth, and the stem cells stored for future use. In October 2006 scientists succeeded in getting umbilical cord stem cells to turn into liver cells. By the end of the year amniotic fluid stem cells had been used to create muscle, bone, fat, blood vessel, nerve and liver cells in the laboratory.

As stem cell research is based on embryos, some groups have moral objections to this research taking place.

WHAT'S NEXT?

In 2007 scientists in the United States made an important breakthrough when they succeeded in using human stem cells to repair badly damaged blood vessels in laboratory animals. First they produced adult stem cells with the ability to develop into blood cells, capillary wall cells and immune cells. When they injected these cells into the animal, they homed in on the site of injury and began to repair the damaged vessels. Further tests will be carried out before the technique is tried out on humans.

In 2007 researchers in Japan and the USA succeeded in getting skin cells from mice to turn back into stem cells. They did this by injecting the cells with a genetically modified virus that carried specially selected genes into the cell. These genes reprogrammed the skin cells making them indistinguishable from embryonic stem cells. If this technique can be developed, it would prevent the need for embryos to be used in stem cell research.

Treating diseases with stem cells

Stem cells are being studied to discover just how a fully-functioning human being develops from a single fertilised egg cell. Stem cells with genetic defects will be used to gain understanding of

A scientist injects modified mouse stem cells into blastocysts. The mice that will be born following this procedure will be used to study the genetic causes of obesity.

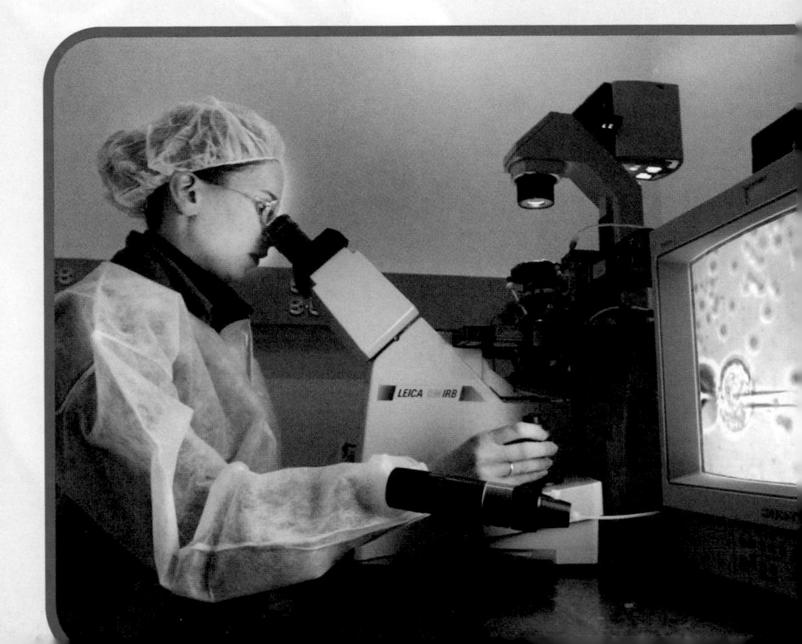

how diseases develop. In the future stem cells may be used to treat many conditions, such as multiple sclerosis, liver damage, Parkinson's disease, Alzheimer's disease, cystic fibrosis and spinal cord injuries.

Growing organs Could we one day grow replacement organs, such as a heart or a kidney, from stem cells? Assuming we can get a supply of stem cells that we know can be turned into the sort of cells we want, how do we get them to grow into the right shape? One way of doing this would be to create a sort of mould or scaffold in the shape of the organ we want to create and encourage the stem cells to grow on it. This could be made from a biodegradable substance that would be broken down by the body when the newly-grown organ was transplanted. Simple organs, such as bladders, have already been grown in this way.

Another use for stem cells is to produce tissues, not for transplant but to be used for drug testing, so avoiding the need to use animals or human volunteers.

The Stem Cell Bank of Andalucía, Spain is the most important stem cell bank in Europe. It will soon reach its goal of 18,000 units of umbilical cord blood stored for a term of two years.

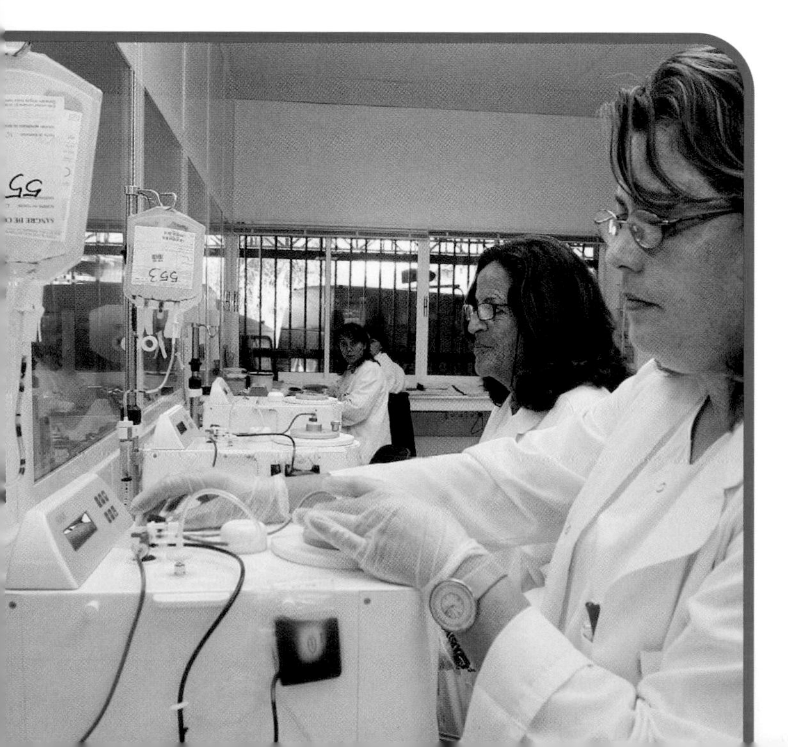

Stem cells and sports In just a few years stem cells from umbilical cord blood might be used in sports medicine, for example for growing new knee ligaments or elbow tendons. In 2007 researchers from the Royal Veterinary College in the United Kingdom developed a technique for treating racehorses. Stem cells are taken from the horse's breastbone and then purified and multiplied in the laboratory. After two or three weeks the stem cells are injected back into the horse's tendon, where they generate new tissue that repairs damage caused by excessive exercise.

No doubt humans will soon follow. Already some sports stars are preparing for the future. Some professional footballers have had their children's stem cells frozen at birth and stored in a Liverpool stem cell bank. Just as stem cells are being used to treat injured horses, so stem cell therapies could be

Repairing injuries in racehorses is only the beginning for a therapy that could lead to the rapid healing of muscle injuries in humans.

WHAT'S NEXT?

Stem cell therapies could be used to build muscles as well as repair them. They could increase stamina by increasing an athlete's red blood cell count. Such enhancements would be practically impossible to detect as the new cells would be just the same as any other cell in the athlete's body. It wouldn't turn a bad athlete into a good one – but it might be enough to turn silver to gold.

used to heal injuries to tendons, ligaments, muscle and cartilage in sports players too. One player described the stem cells as a potential repair kit for a career-threatening injury. Some researchers think this type of treatment will be available in the next few years.

Problems to solve In the same way that a transplant patient's body may reject a donated organ, there is also the possibility that donated stem cells will be rejected by the patient. Collecting healthy adult stem cells from a patient and stimulating them in the laboratory to create the type of tissue needed would solve this problem. The tissue would be grown and then transplanted into the patient's body to take the place of the lost or damaged tissue.

Stem cells and cloning A great deal of research is going into the possibility of making embryonic stem cells using the same techniques that have been used to produce cloned animals. There are many technical problems to be overcome before this method of producing stem cells becomes a reality.

HOW IT WORKS

In cloning, a cell – a muscle or skin cell, for example – is taken from a patient. The nucleus, the part of the cell that contains the genetic material, is removed from the cell and injected into an unfertilised egg that has had its own nucleus removed. The egg, which now contains the patient's genetic material, is treated with chemicals or an electric current to get it to begin dividing and form an embryo. The stem cells that form in the embryo will each contain a copy of the patient's DNA and so will any tissues they form. Because they are genetically identical to the patient's own cells they will not be rejected by the patient's body.

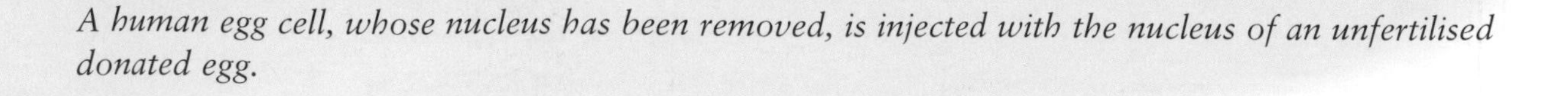

A human egg cell, whose nucleus has been removed, is injected with the nucleus of an unfertilised donated egg.

Using animal eggs Research is under way to produce human stem cells using the eggs of other animals. Scientists will use eggs from rabbits or cows. The nucleus of a patient with a genetic illness, such as cystic fibrosis, will replace the nucleus of the animal egg. The embryo produced will provide stem cells that will be used to study how the illness progresses and to test drugs to cure it. Because the animal's genetic material has been removed there is absolutely no danger of the embryo becoming a human-animal hybrid. It will be genetically the same as the human donor.

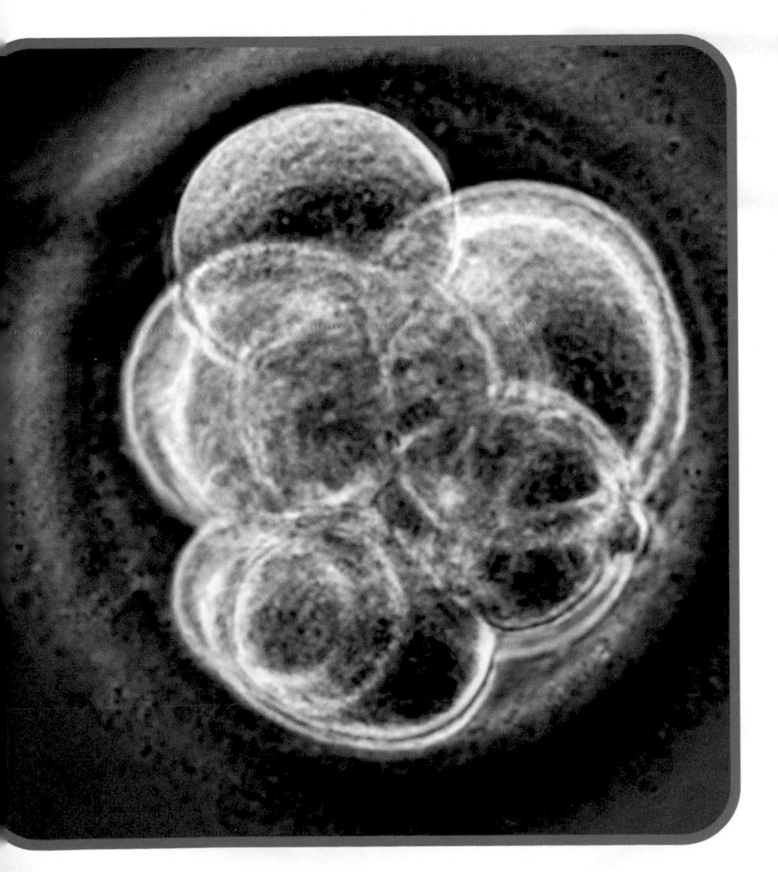

FOR AND AGAINST

For

- Stem cells can be used to test new medications for safety and effectiveness without using animals or human volunteers.
- Stem cells can be used to repair cells or tissues that have been damaged by disease or injury.
- Stem cells might one day be used to grow entire organs for transplantation.

Against

- Obtaining stem cells from human embryos is highly controversial. For many people, each embryo represents a potential human life and to use them in this way is akin to murder.
- Producing stem cells by cloning also poses problems. In theory, the embryo could be implanted into a woman's womb where it might develop into a cloned human baby.
- There is some evidence that stem cells in the body dividing uncontrollably are one of the main causes of cancer.

A three-day old cloned human embryo, created at the Centre for Life in Newcastle upon Tyne, England. The blastocyst was created by inserting DNA into an unfertilised human egg.

CHAPTER 6
nanotech medicine

Nanotechnology is about the manipulation and manufacture of materials and devices on the scale of atoms and molecules. A nanometre is one billionth of a metre. To give you an idea how small that is, a single red blood cell would be about 5,000 nanometres across and a single human hair about 80,000 nanometres. This is technology at the cutting edge and practical results may not emerge for some years, but there are amazing possibilities for medicine.

Nanocrystals Quantum dots, also called nanocrystals, are a type of material known as a semiconductor. Semiconductors are widely used in electronics as important parts of circuit boards and microchips. Nanocrystals are extremely small, ranging from 2-10 nanometres in diameter. Three million nanocrystals would fit across your thumb.

Nano drugs Nano-sized drug particles could revolutionise the way we take medicines. They could be made to seek out a site of disease so the drug is delivered to precisely the right part of the body and engineered to release drug doses exactly as required.

Many diseases affect processes that take place inside the cells of the body,

The nanoparticles created by scientists at the University of Michigan, USA. These nanoparticles have two sides. Each side can have a different function.

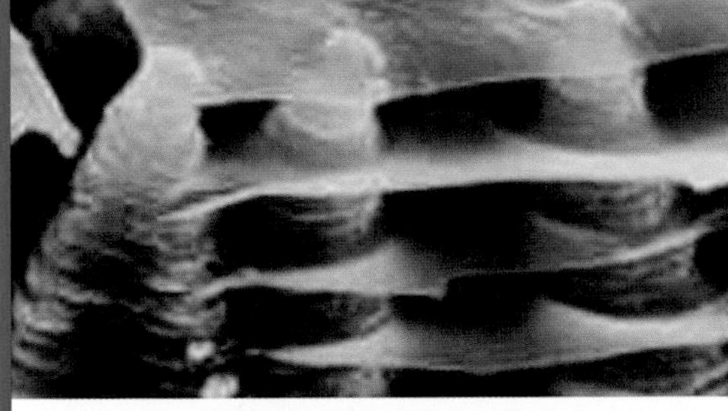

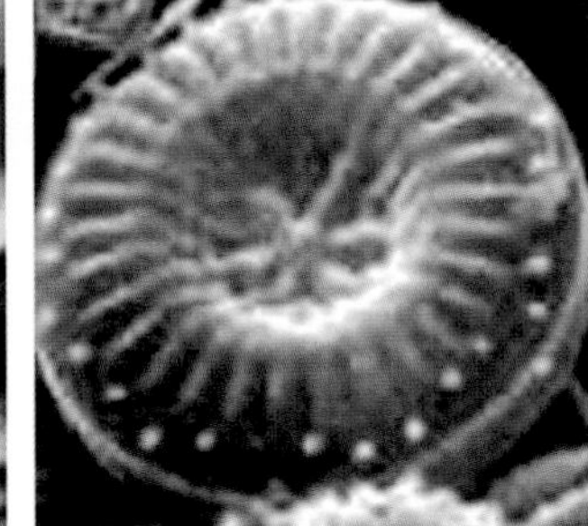

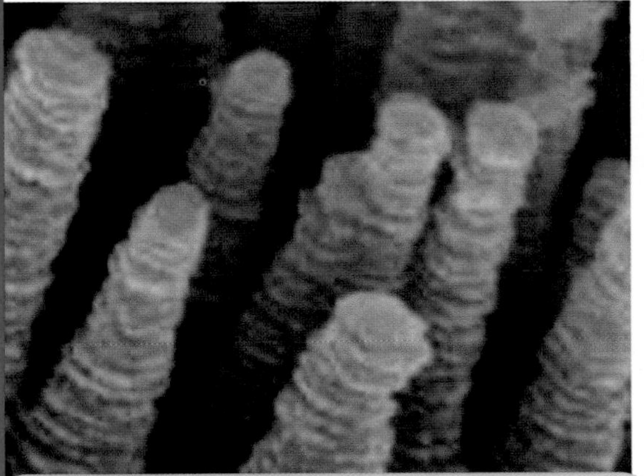

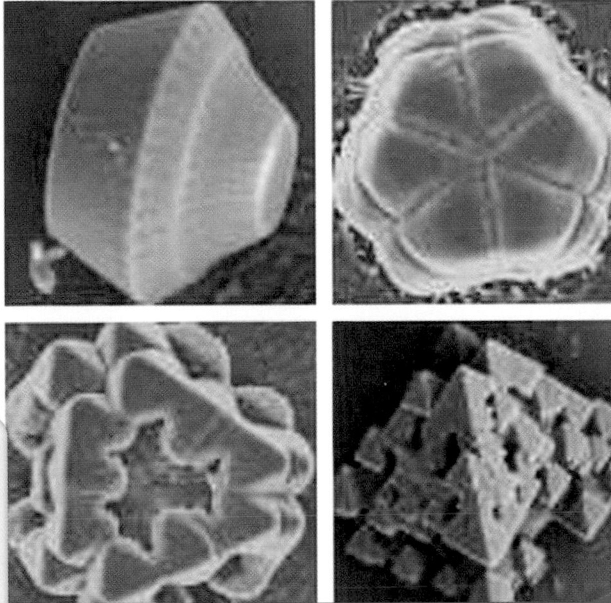

There are different types of nanocrystals. Their shape is affected by growth conditions that can be controlled.

HOW IT WORKS

Nanocrystals are like tiny beads that can be made to give off light. Using this technology could revolutionise medical imaging and the detection of disease. One of the first uses of nanotechnology in medicine came in 2005 when researchers at Vanderbilt University in the United States made nanocrystals that attached themselves to a particular type of virus. By detecting the glow from the nanocrystals they were able to find the disease-causing virus in just a few hours, rather than the two to five days that conventional detection methods take. This meant that they knew exactly how to treat the patient.

so drug delivery mechanisms are being developed that will include the ability to get drugs through cell walls and into cells where they can do most good. Because nanoparticles are so small, the body's cells take them up more readily. Often the body will get rid of drugs before they have been absorbed into the cells where they are needed. The result of this is that the patient has to take higher doses of the drug, with the possibility of unwanted side effects.

Nanoparticles could solve this problem by being triggered to release the drugs they carry only when they encounter the cells that need the drugs.

Jeff Brinker (left) and Hongyou Fan observe their fluorescent nanocrystals in water solution. The dark vial holds gold nanocrystals; the orange and green are semiconductor nanocrystals.

Nanosensors A sensor is a device for detecting changes in its surroundings – changes in temperature, light, pressure, concentrations of chemicals, and so on – and which signals these changes to a monitoring device. Incredibly fine tubes of carbon just one or two nanometres in diameter – called nanotubes – could be

used to make sensors of great sensitivity, known as nanosensors. Research is currently under way to find ways of using these nanotubes in a number of medical devices. Another possibility is the use of silicon-based nanowires.

A nanosensor can detect changes on a very small scale and could, for example, be used to detect cancer tumours of only a few cells, which could be easily dealt with before they became dangerous. Nanowires could be used as very sensitive virus detectors, spotting infection before it has a chance to take hold.

Nanotech eyes In early 2007 researchers at the University of Texas Medical Branch and the University of Michigan succeeded in making the world's first direct electrical link between nerve cells and miniscule nanoparticles with the ability to turn light into tiny electrical currents that can produce responses in nerves. The exciting thing about this development is that it opens up the possibility of a nanoparticle-based artificial retina (the part of the eye that detects light signals and passes them on to the brain) being produced in the future.

The future The researchers believe that it should be possible to tune the electrical characteristics of the nanoparticle films to get properties like colour sensitivity and to give different responses to varying light levels. The light-sensitive nanoparticle-nerve cell link shows great promise but the day when an actual artificial retina can be safely installed in someone's eye is probably still several years off.

Fantastic voyage Around 40 years ago, a science fiction movie called *Fantastic Voyage* imagined a team of doctors being shrunk down to a size smaller than a cell

HOW IT WORKS

To create a nanotech eye, the Texas and Michigan scientists built a layer-by-layer sandwich on a glass plate using two kinds of ultra-thin film, one made of mercury-tellurium nanoparticles and another of a polymer called PDDA. On top of this sandwich went a layer of clay and a coating of amino acid (amino acids are the building blocks of proteins and are found in all living things). Finally there came a layer of nerve cells that had been cultured in the laboratory.

When light shines on the nanoparticle layers they produce electrons, which then move up into the PDDA layers and produce an electrical current. When the current reaches the nerve cells it stimulates them into firing off a signal.

and injected into a patient's bloodstream in a miniature submarine. While we could never go there in person, the next best thing would be to send robots and cameras inside the body. Researchers in the NanoRobotics Laboratory of École Polytechnique de Montréal's Department of Computer Engineering and Institute of Biomedical Engineering in Canada achieved a major technological breakthrough in 2007. They succeeded for the first time in guiding, via computer control, a microdevice inside

HOW IT WORKS

The research team injected a magnetised sphere 1.5 millimetres in diameter into the carotid artery of an animal placed inside an MRI scanner. They were able to steer it using computer programs that adjusted the magnetic field of the scanner to move the sphere.

Researcher Sylvain Martel with colleagues at the NanoRobotics Laboratory of Montréal who created the microdevice.

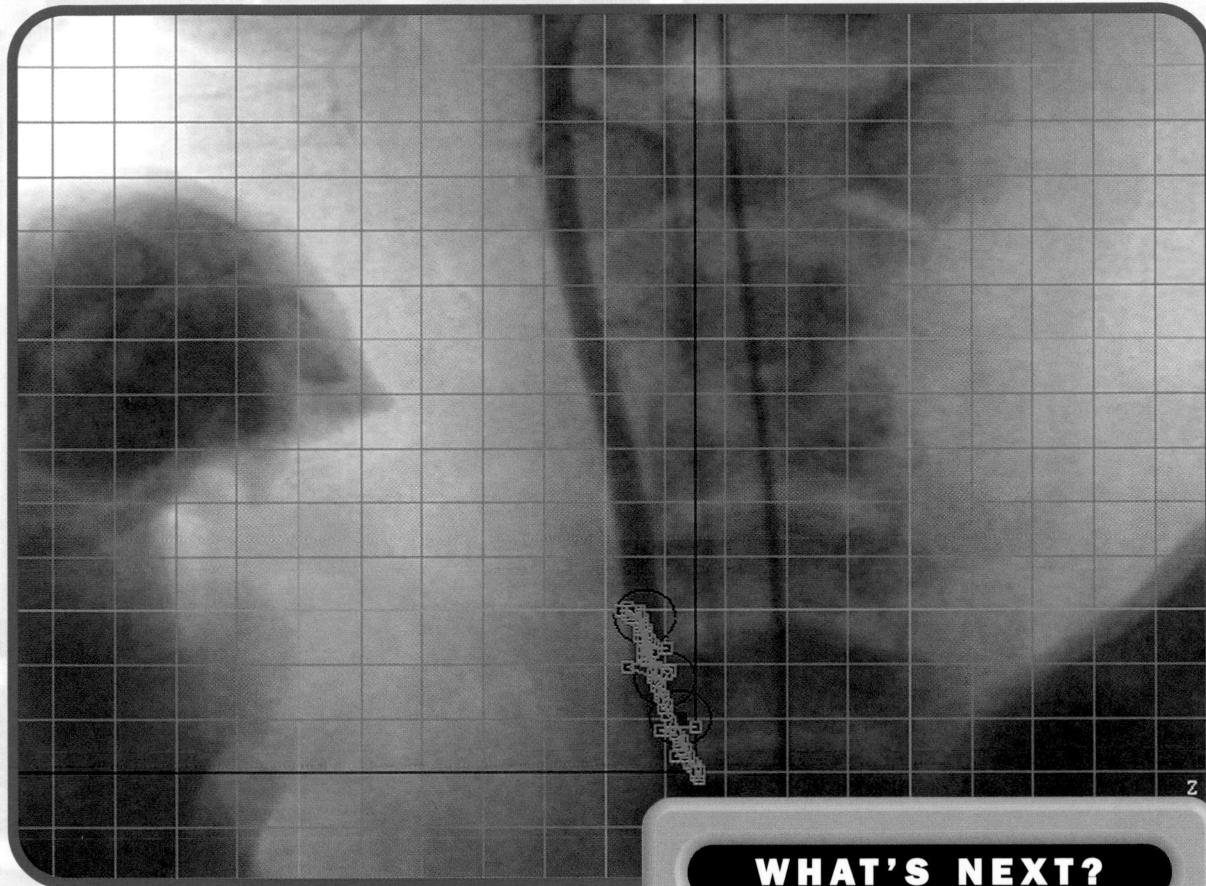

The microdevice created by the NanoRobotics Laboratory as it travelled along the artery of a pig.

an artery of a living animal. The device travelled at a very respectable speed of 10 centimetres per second.

Possible uses The human body contains nearly 100,000 kilometres of blood vessels. Injection and control of microdevices inside the blood vessels could enable treatment to be given at specific target sites in the body that are hard to get at using current medical instruments.

WHAT'S NEXT?

Staff at the NanoRobotics Laboratory are currently working to reduce the size of their devices so that they can navigate inside smaller blood vessels. Researchers are developing several types of microdevices that could be used, for example, to deliver medications directly to tumour sites and to diagnose disease using bio-sensors that could be sent to investigate areas of concern.

CHAPTER 7

into the future

Advances in medicine can take unexpected and surprising directions. Here are some examples of surprising innovations.

One of the major causes of death is cancer. It is a disease in which some cells in the body begin to grow and multiply uncontrollably, causing damage to surrounding tissues.

Scientists working in the United States have made an unusual breakthrough in the fight against this illness. They have created a paint that will allow surgeons to see cancer cells 500 times better than they can using current technology.

HOW IT WORKS

Researchers at the Seattle Children's Hospital Research Institute and the Fred Hutchinson Cancer Research Centre created the paint. It uses a chemical, called chlorotoxin, which is obtained from scorpions. This chemical glows when seen under infrared light. The paint attaches itself to tumour cells but not normal cells and will help surgeons see where a tumour begins and ends more accurately than was possible before.

Cancerous cells are illuminated by chlorotoxin, the main chemical in the newly-developed cancer paint.

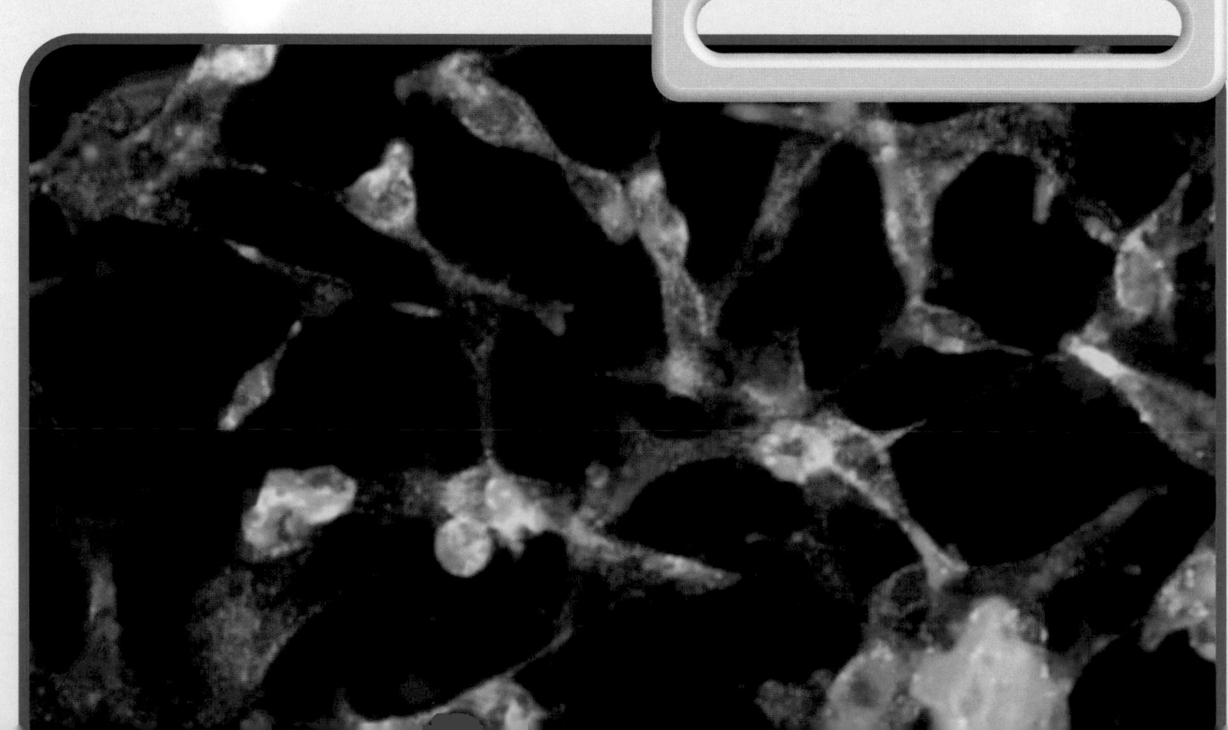

Current technology, such as magnetic resonance imaging, can distinguish tumours from healthy tissue only if more than a million cancer cells are present. But chlorotoxin could be used to identify tumours with as few as 2,000 cancer cells, which makes it 500 times more sensitive than MRI.

Some researchers think more work needs to be done to discover why chlorotoxin binds to tumour cells and not normal cells. It is also important to make sure that the paint has no dangerous side effects before it is cleared for use on humans. All being well the paint might be used in operating theatres by 2009.

A brain scan by a tomography system which displays colour-coded 'slices' of the brain. Ever more powerful computers make such images possible.

Combining skills Medical research and development is proceeding rapidly on many fronts and making use of all the technical ability we have available to us. More and more, developments in medical technology come from co-operation between people with many different skills. Medicine, science, computer programming and engineering will all come together to provide the healthcare of the future.

The power of computers will no doubt play a big part in the future. Not only thanks to their ability to visualise such things as complex three dimensional models of potential new drugs, but also because they are making it easier to share ideas more rapidly than ever before.

glossary

amniotic fluid A watery liquid surrounding and cushioning a foetus while inside its mother's womb.

antibiotics Substances produced by certain fungi, bacteria and other organisms which block the growth or kill bacteria that cause disease.

bacteria Tiny organisms that sometimes cause disease.

bionic The use of mechanical equipment to replace a part of the body.

bone marrow The material inside bones; a complex mixture of cells which produces the body's blood; also contains a form of stem cell to help repair the body when injured.

capillary wall cells The cells that make up the walls of the tiny blood vessels that connect arteries and veins.

chemotherapy A therapy for cancer using chemicals.

cloning The process of making an identical copy of a living thing.

DNA Short for deoxyribonucleic acid, a molecule that contains the genetic instructions for how a living being lives and grows.

electrode An electric connector through which an electric current passes.

embryo An unborn baby up to eight weeks after conception.

enzyme Substance that speeds up chemical reactions in living things.

foetus Unborn baby after the eighth week of conception.

gene A segment of DNA which can produce, or control the production of, a specific biological molecule. Genes are grouped into chromosomes within the cell and are inherited.

insulin A hormone that controls blood glucose levels.

IVF Short for 'in-vitro ('in glass') fertilisation', when an embryo is produced outside the body.

leukaemia A cancer of the blood or bone marrow.

microprocessor A computer processor contained on an integrated-circuit chip, sometimes called a computer chip.

molecule Particle made from two or more atoms joined together.

parasite A plant or animal that lives off another in a way that harms or weakens it.

placenta An organ that develops during pregnancy in mammals, which provides the baby with food and oxygen.

polymer Large molecules made from smaller identical molecules joined end to end.

prostheses Artificial replacements for parts of the body such as limbs or teeth.

semiconductors Materials that allow electricity to pass through them gradually. Silicon is often used to make semiconductors.

stamina Ability to endure physical stress.

stem cells Cells that are able to renew themselves and that are able to develop into other different types of cells.

umbilical cord The cord that connects the developing foetus to the placenta, bringing nourishment to the foetus and removing wastes.

virus A tiny particle that can infect the cells of living things. Viruses can only multiply once they have infected a cell.

further information

Books

Technology all around us: Medicine by Kristina Routh, Franklin Watts, 2005.

21st Century Science: Medicine by Robin Kerrod, Smart Apple Media, 2006.

Websites

http://science.howstuffworks.com/stem-cell.htm

Easy to understand guide to genetic research sponsored by GlaxoSmithKline
http://www.genetics.gsk.com/kids/index_kids.htm

http://www.sciencenewsforkids.org/

Places to visit

Royal London Museum
The Royal London Hospital
St Augustine with St Philip's Church
Newark Street
London E1 2AA
http://www.bartsandthelondon.nhs.uk/aboutus/royallondonhospitalmuseum.asp

Science Museum
Exhibition Road
South Kensington
London SW7 2DD
http://www.sciencemuseum.org.uk/

Thinktank
Birmingham Science Museum
Millennium Point
Curzon Street
Birmingham, B4 7XG
http://www.thinktank.ac
Medical exhibitions include Things About Me and Medicine Matters.

Thackray Museum
Beckett Street
Leeds
LS9 7LN
http://www.thackraymuseum.org/

index

Numbers in *italic* refer to illustrations.